RATTLESNAKE
DANCE

RATTLESNAKE DANCE

TRUE TALES, MYSTERIES, AND RATTLESNAKE CEREMONIES

Jennifer Owings Dewey

Boyds Mills Press

For my friend,

Don MacCarter

Copyright © 1997 by Jennifer Owings Dewey
All Rights Reserved

Published by Caroline House
Boyds Mills Press, Inc.
A Highlights Company
815 Church Street
Honesdale, Pennsylvania 18431
Printed in China

Publisher Cataloging-in-Publication Data
Dewey, Jennifer Owings.
Rattlesnake Dance / by Jennifer Owings Dewey.--1st ed.
[48]p.: Col. Ill.; CM.
Summary: Facts and Folk Beliefs About Rattlesnakes Accompany an Autobiographical
Account of Three Personal Encounters With Rattlesnakes.
ISBN 1-56397-247-6 HC • ISBN 1-56397-877-6 PBK
1. Rattlesnakes--Fiction--Juvenile Literature. 2. Snakes--Fiction--Juvenile Literature
[1. Rattlesnakes--Fiction. 2. Snakes--Fiction.] I. Title.
597.96 [E]--DC20 1997 AC CIP
Library of Congress Catalog Card Number 96-84170

First edition, 1997
Book Designed by Jeanne Abboud
The Text of This Book is Set in 12.5 Berkeley Medium
The Illustrations are Done in Colored Pencil

10 9 8 7 6 5 4 3 HC
10 9 8 7 6 5 4 3 2 1 PBK

CONTENTS

TIGER

Arizona
Mexico

BLACKTAIL

Arizona
New Mexico
Texas
Mexico

PIGMY

Alabama
Arkansas
District of Columbia
Kentucky
Louisiana
Mississippi
Missouri
North Carolina
Oklahoma
South Carolina
Texas
Virginia
West Virginia
Canada

MASSASAUGA

Arizona	*Nebraska*
Colorado	*New Mexico*
Illinois	*New York*
Indiana	*Ohio*
Iowa	*Oklahoma*
Kansas	*Texas*
Louisiana	*Wisconsin*
Michigan	*Mexico*
Minnesota	

SPECIES OF

Fifteen primary species of rattlesnakes live in the United States. The map below shows the states in which they are commonly found. Many subspecies

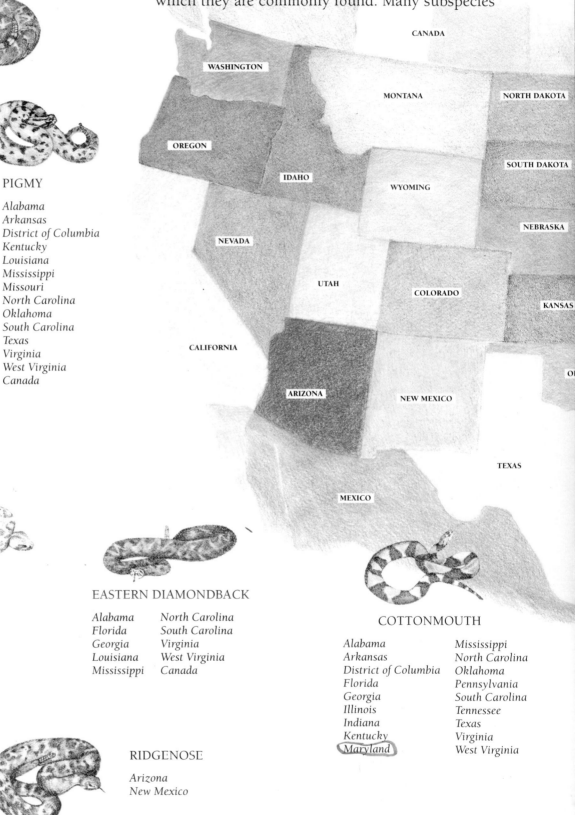

WESTERN
DIAMONDBACK

Arizona
Arkansas
California
Nevada
New Mexico
Oklahoma
Texas
Utah
Mexico

RED DIAMOND

California
Mexico

EASTERN DIAMONDBACK

Alabama	*North Carolina*
Florida	*South Carolina*
Georgia	*Virginia*
Louisiana	*West Virginia*
Mississippi	*Canada*

RIDGENOSE

Arizona
New Mexico

COTTONMOUTH

Alabama	*Mississippi*
Arkansas	*North Carolina*
District of Columbia	*Oklahoma*
Florida	*Pennsylvania*
Georgia	*South Carolina*
Illinois	*Tennessee*
Indiana	*Texas*
Kentucky	*Virginia*
Maryland	*West Virginia*

RATTLESNAKES

exist, however, and among these is the prairie rattlesnake—the subspecies mentioned in Part I and Part III of this book. The copperhead and the cottonmouth are shown as well; both are pit vipers, like rattlesnakes, but have no rattles.

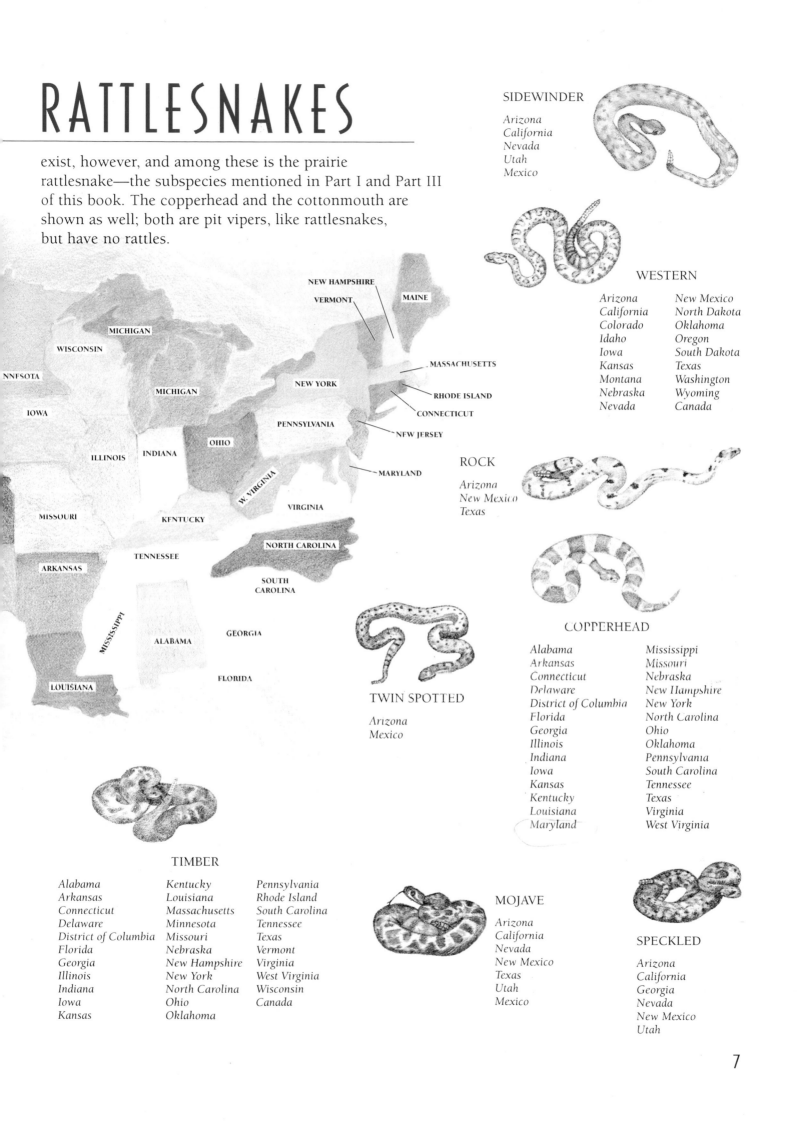

SIDEWINDER

Arizona
California
Nevada
Utah
Mexico

WESTERN

Arizona	*New Mexico*
California	*North Dakota*
Colorado	*Oklahoma*
Idaho	*Oregon*
Iowa	*South Dakota*
Kansas	*Texas*
Montana	*Washington*
Nebraska	*Wyoming*
Nevada	*Canada*

ROCK

Arizona
New Mexico
Texas

COPPERHEAD

Alabama	*Mississippi*
Arkansas	*Missouri*
Connecticut	*Nebraska*
Delaware	*New Hampshire*
District of Columbia	*New York*
Florida	*North Carolina*
Georgia	*Ohio*
Illinois	*Oklahoma*
Indiana	*Pennsylvania*
Iowa	*South Carolina*
Kansas	*Tennessee*
Kentucky	*Texas*
Louisiana	*Virginia*
Maryland	*West Virginia*

TWIN SPOTTED

Arizona
Mexico

TIMBER

Alabama	*Kentucky*	*Pennsylvania*
Arkansas	*Louisiana*	*Rhode Island*
Connecticut	*Massachusetts*	*South Carolina*
Delaware	*Minnesota*	*Tennessee*
District of Columbia	*Missouri*	*Texas*
Florida	*Nebraska*	*Vermont*
Georgia	*New Hampshire*	*Virginia*
Illinois	*New York*	*West Virginia*
Indiana	*North Carolina*	*Wisconsin*
Iowa	*Ohio*	*Canada*
Kansas	*Oklahoma*	

MOJAVE

Arizona
California
Nevada
New Mexico
Texas
Utah
Mexico

SPECKLED

Arizona
California
Georgia
Nevada
New Mexico
Utah

7

SNAKEBITE

W hen I was nine years old, I climbed up a cliff face on a sandstone ridge in the hills north of the ranch where I lived in New Mexico.

While reaching over my head for a grip on a ledge, I felt the strike. There was stunning pain from the instant the twin fangs pierced the soft, fleshy side of my hand. It felt as if a pair of needles had been driven into my body.

I used to ride into the hills all the time, usually alone. I'd dismount and explore, trying to find new ways to the tops of the cliffs. My horse waited on the flats below, her reins looped over a piñon or juniper branch.

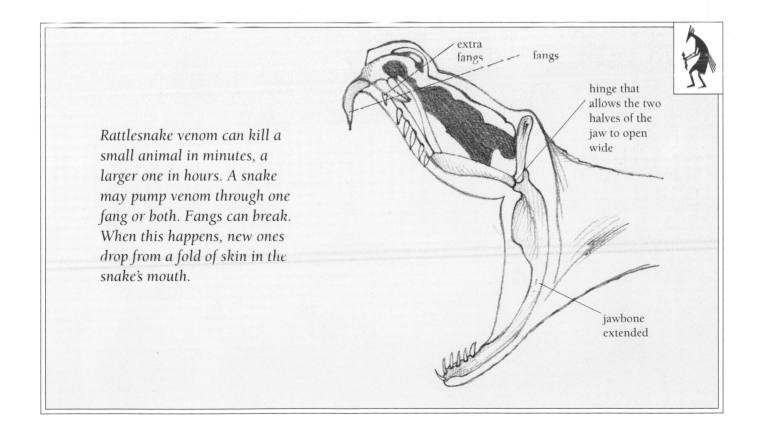

Rattlesnake venom can kill a small animal in minutes, a larger one in hours. A snake may pump venom through one fang or both. Fangs can break. When this happens, new ones drop from a fold of skin in the snake's mouth.

extra
fangs

fangs

hinge that
allows the two
halves of the
jaw to open
wide

jawbone
extended

In the fraction of a second the snake took to strike, it buzzed its rattle. My horse did not hear the sound. If she had, she'd have bolted. She feared snakes as much as most horses do.

I slid like a rag doll down the slope. I swung onto my horse's back and turned for home, clamping my good hand around a swatch of her mane. I held on as if my life depended on it.

I urged my horse to a run, beating her sides with my heels. She was old and lazy and hated running.

The Navajo Indians believe that the spirit of a mean person is likely to be lodged in the body of a rattlesnake.

Some venoms have a gyrotoxic effect, which causes prey to twist and spin in chaotic circles. As the animal reels across the ground, it leaves its scent on everything it touches. The snake has a trail to follow as it goes after its meal.

Rattlesnakes are pit vipers, named for the pits on each side of their heads. The pits are lined with heat-sensitive cells. These cells are strong enough to lead a snake to its prey in complete darkness. If you blindfold a pit viper, it will still hit its mark in a strike.

heat-sensing pits

Ten minutes into the twenty-minute ride my stomach backed up and I started feeling dizzy. I was afraid of falling off the horse. The earth and sky rotated. Blue mountains in the distance reeled and rolled. My vision began to cloud over. Black shadows moved across my eyes until all I could see was a tiny pinpoint of light.

I wondered if I'd make it home before I died.

My horse's reluctant lope finally brought us to the main gate of the ranch. I slid off her back and somehow got the gate open. A few more stumbling steps and I came to the big corral. Lucky for me, Bill, the ranch foreman, was there.

Reaching his side I blurted out, "A rattlesnake bit me," before slumping to the ground.

"Good lord," Bill exclaimed. I couldn't see his face. His voice described his shock at the sight of me. "How in the world…?"

Bill lifted me in his arms and carried me. In a tight, strained voice he said, "I thought I told you how to keep clear of those critters. I figured you knew better than to get yourself snakebit."

He wasn't scolding. It was his fear talking. He was wondering if I would die.

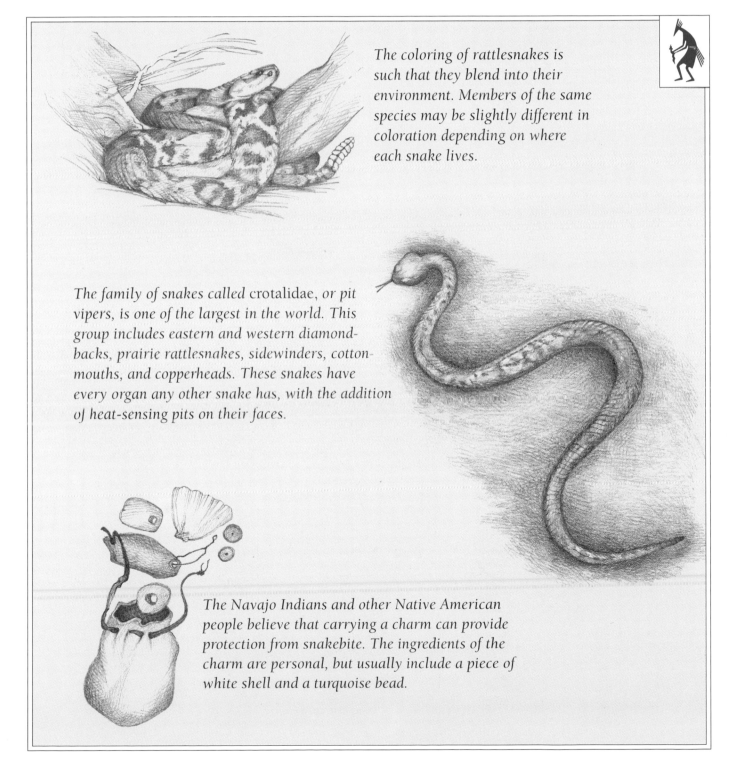

The coloring of rattlesnakes is such that they blend into their environment. Members of the same species may be slightly different in coloration depending on where each snake lives.

The family of snakes called crotalidae, *or pit vipers, is one of the largest in the world. This group includes eastern and western diamond-backs, prairie rattlesnakes, sidewinders, cotton-mouths, and copperheads. These snakes have every organ any other snake has, with the addition of heat-sensing pits on their faces.*

The Navajo Indians and other Native American people believe that carrying a charm can provide protection from snakebite. The ingredients of the charm are personal, but usually include a piece of white shell and a turquoise bead.

We came to the Chevy pickup and Bill got the door open. He slid me onto the seat, and I screamed. My hand, arm, and shoulder pulsed with a knifelike pain that started in my fingers and shot to my brain. The dizziness got worse. I could still see nothing but a single bead of light.

What makes rattlesnake venom deadly is the reptile's delivery system — the fact that a rattlesnake injects its venom directly into the flesh. Venom is made up of protein enzymes, as is human saliva. Enzymes break down tissue and bone. In a strike, venom flows through fangs, which act as hypodermic needles. Inside the prey, venom starts the process of digestion.

Arizona

Most rattlesnakes live in warm climates. In the United States, Arizona has the most rattlesnakes — with eleven species. Maine has no rattlesnakes; Washington and Oregon have only one species.
Rattlesnakes tend to live in areas where they are not likely to be bothered by people.

People once believed venoms were destructive to either blood or nerves. Now it is understood that venoms can be deadly because they affect both the circulatory system and nerve tissue.

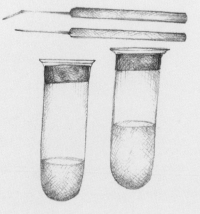

Indians in northern Mexico once believed that the best way to cure snakebite was to cover the afflicted limb in the earth until the pain stopped.

Bill drove full tilt up the dirt road to the ranch house.
He slammed to a stop by the kitchen door.

"Got to tell someone what happened," he said, jump-
ing out.

"Don't go," I whispered, trying to follow.

"Got to," he said. "Be right back."

He was back in seconds, but it felt like forever.

If rattlesnake venom is swallowed as if it were a glass of water, it is completely harmless — unless the person drinking it has a mouth sore or an ulcer.

In the split second of a strike — too fast to be followed by the human eye — a rattlesnake's sense organs collect information about the prey. With this "chemical memory" fixed in its brain, the snake can track its victim. When the prey is dead, the snake swallows it whole.

On the way to town, seventeen miles away, I was sick. Bill stopped the truck so I could throw up. He held me by the waist at the side of the road because I couldn't stand alone.

I stayed conscious for a while after that, until the effort became too great. It felt as though my body were floating away, taking the pain with it.

Rattlesnake venom is similiar to saliva in other animals, including humans. If human saliva were injected into another animal—a rattlesnake for example—the snake might suffer a near-fatal allergic reaction. Rattlesnakes have no immunity to human saliva, and we have none to their venom. Because rattlesnake venom is highly concentrated, compared to human saliva, the introduction of venom into human tissue is extremely dangerous.

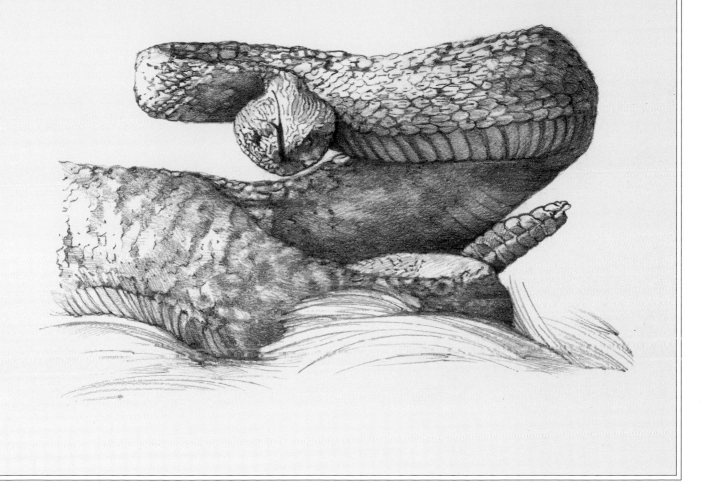

"Looks like a prairie got her," the doctor said. "But it might have been a western diamondback. The venoms have a similar effect."

The doctor directed his words to Bill, not to me. I lay on a smooth, stainless-steel surface in the hospital emergency room. My vision was changing again. The pinpoint of light was getting wider with every minute that passed.

"Can you give her antivenin? Can you treat her?"

"We don't have any antivenin," the doctor said, his voice as slick as the table I lay on.

"I don't understand," Bill said.

"The hospital is out of antivenin right now. There are measures we can take to treat her, but we're out of serum."

"She's just a kid," Bill protested, sounding angry and afraid. "Just a skinny kid."

"I've seen folks pull through snakebite," the doctor said. "Even kids."

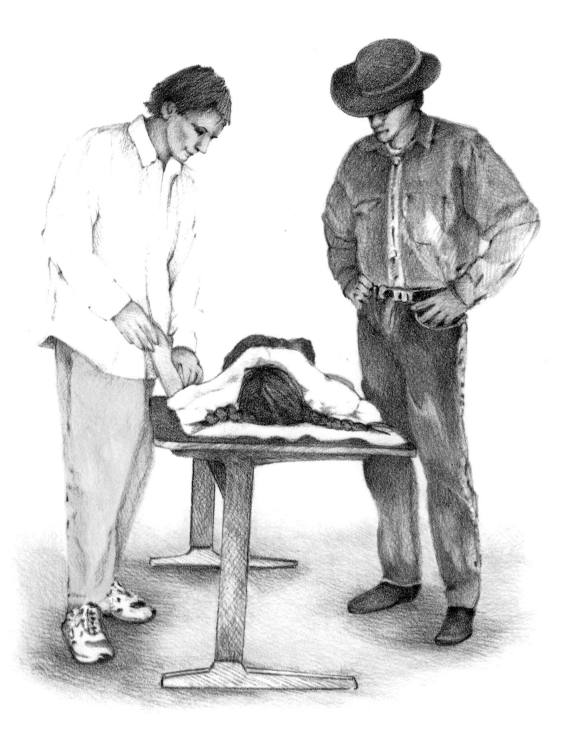

My brain spun and whirled the way a planet does.
The light in the room expanded. My vision was so
wide I couldn't tell where the edges of things were. Then
fear, and the anguish of pain, made me pass out again.

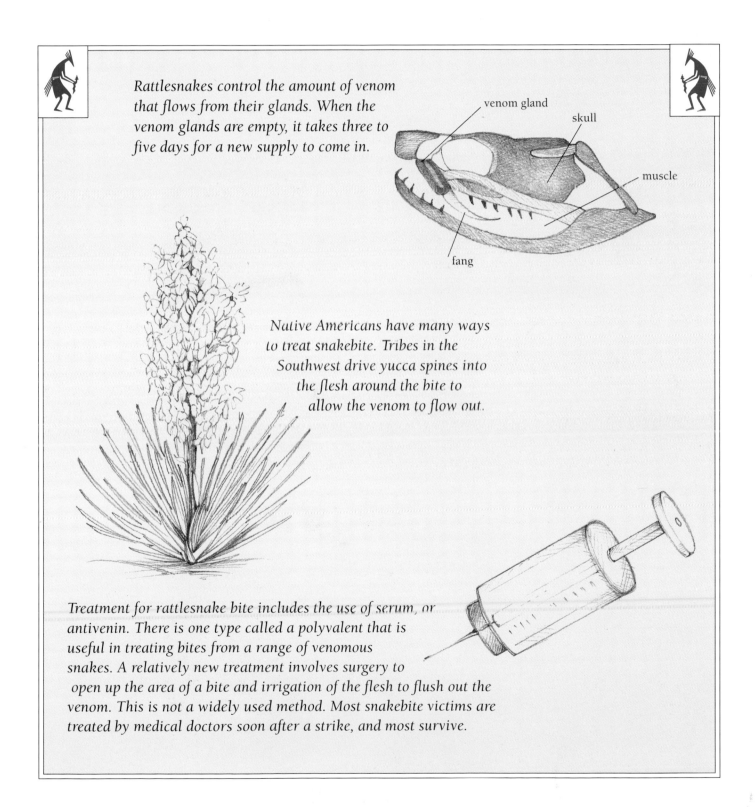

Rattlesnakes control the amount of venom
that flows from their glands. When the
venom glands are empty, it takes three to
five days for a new supply to come in.

venom gland

skull

muscle

fang

Native Americans have many ways
to treat snakebite. Tribes in the
Southwest drive yucca spines into
the flesh around the bite to
allow the venom to flow out.

Treatment for rattlesnake bite includes the use of serum, or
antivenin. There is one type called a polyvalent that is
useful in treating bites from a range of venomous
snakes. A relatively new treatment involves surgery to
open up the area of a bite and irrigation of the flesh to flush out the
venom. This is not a widely used method. Most snakebite victims are
treated by medical doctors soon after a strike, and most survive.

I remained unconscious, for the most part, for three days. I experienced some awareness. I knew Bill stayed. My parents came. I caught glimpses of faces, and I heard voices. Everything came through a mist of persistent, burning pain. In moments of consciousness, my mind was focused on the agony in my limbs. Nothing else was real.

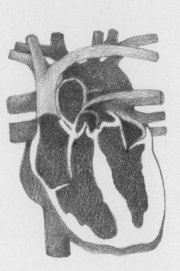

Pharmaceutical companies use venom, diluted and mixed with other chemical compounds, to make medications for humans. One example is heart medicine. Venom in the body alters the rate of blood flow and the frequency of heartbeat. Under special circumstances, venom is useful for people with heart disease.

An old-time folk remedy for snakebite was snakeweed, or hierba de vibora. Some people said you made a tea and drank it. Others mashed the root to a pulp and applied this to the wound. Still others said the best method was to rub the mashed root into the bite and drink the tea at the same time.

Overheated rattlesnake venom is less potent because it is warm. Venom can be chilled, or even frozen, without altering its potency.

When I was awake I looked at the snakebit side of my body. The swelling was astonishing. My skin was shiny and purplish-black. The tightness of it made me wonder if I might explode.

Red streaks traveled like marks on a road map over my chest and right arm. It hurt to have a sheet on me. I was feverish, and it was impossible to keep food down.

A famous folktale describes how a rattlesnake bit a wagon tongue, which swelled up so badly the driver chopped it off with his axe to save his wagon.

No matter what the effects of venom are on a human victim, there is always massive swelling, as well as necrosis, the decay and death of healthy tissue. The discoloration of skin in the area of a bite is caused by both the swelling and necrosis.

My first full day of consciousness was the fourth day after the strike. I had no feeling in my fingertips, toes, or the skin of my scalp.

"You're doing great," the doctor said on one of his visits to my room. "You can go home soon."

"Home? You mean I'm going to live?"

"Looks that way," the doctor said, smiling. "We have some work to do, but you can go home in the meantime."

By "work" the doctor meant skin grafts, three in all, to replace ulcerated skin at the site of the bite.

About 8,000 people a year are struck by pit vipers in North America. Of this number, ten to fifteen die. More people are killed by lightning storms. Common snakebite victims are young children and people who handle snakes for religious purposes or sport.

According to Micmac Indian legend, thunder was made by seven rattlesnakes flying across the sky, crying out to each other and flinging their tails about. Lightning was created when the snakes dove to the earth after prey.

Before leaving the hospital, I asked the doctor if he thought he knew what sort of snake had struck me.

"I believe it was a prairie," he said. "And I suspect you didn't get the full volume of venom the snake had in its glands. Otherwise I don't think you'd have made it."

I pictured a prairie rattlesnake basking on the ledge in the hills where I'd climbed. It was no wonder the snake struck, with a human hand suddenly thrust into its face.

Back home, I rested in a lawn chair in the yard for most of the summer. I was too tired to do much but read and sleep. Three weeks to the day after the strike, the swelling was confined to my right hand and arm, up to my elbow. The purple-black skin peeled away like scales falling off a butterfly's wing.

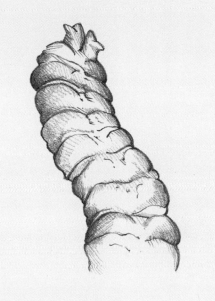

I slowly regained strength. The trips to town for skin grafts were scary at first, but I soon realized there was nothing to be afraid of. The doctor took tiny patches of skin from my backside and layered them over the wound on my hand. In time it was almost impossible to tell that I'd ever been bitten.

HOPI SNAKE CEREMONIES

Death is not the automatic result of a snakebite. I learned this when I was nine. But the mystery of snakebite and venom, and the human response to these, deepened for me when I was ten and my father took me to the Hopi snake ceremonies in Arizona.

For more than two weeks in August the Hopi Indians held secret rituals that concluded with the snake dance. On those days non-Indians were allowed to watch the dance, although they probably understood little of what they saw. My father did his best to explain what he knew.

People have believed rattlesnakes are capable of charming birds out of the sky simply by staring hard and hypnotizing the birds until they drop to the ground.

The Hopi live in a bone-dry region of the desert Southwest. They depend on rain to water their crops. The Hopi believe snakes have unique powers, that they are messengers between humans and spirits — especially the spirits that bring the rain.

For the Hopi, the snake ceremony is a time to make a plea to the spirits for the water the Indians badly need to survive.

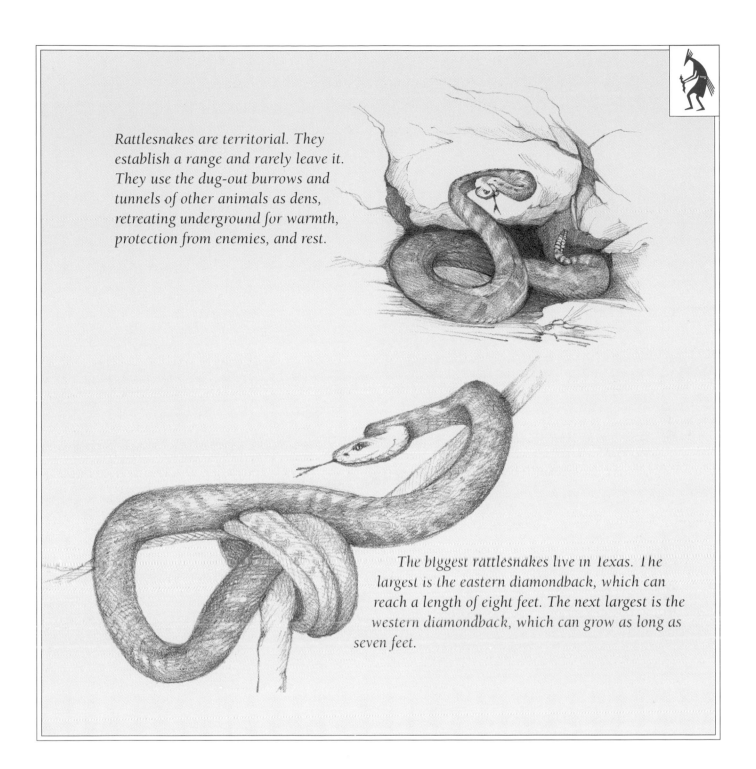

Rattlesnakes are territorial. They establish a range and rarely leave it. They use the dug-out burrows and tunnels of other animals as dens, retreating underground for warmth, protection from enemies, and rest.

The biggest rattlesnakes live in Texas. The largest is the eastern diamondback, which can reach a length of eight feet. The next largest is the western diamondback, which can grow as long as seven feet.

We drove to Hopi country in the pickup truck and camped in a dry arroyo. We then hiked up a steep trail to a village on a mesa-top, a Hopi town. The dance started in the late afternoon under a cloudless blue sky.

The dancers, all men, filed into the dance plaza of the town. They had shoulder-length hair as sleek and black as raven wings. Bunches of eagle feathers were tied into the thick strands.

The men were painted black and white, with zig-zag lines to represent lightning. They wore knee-length kilts and woven belts. Each of the dancers had a tortoise-shell rattle tied to his right leg below the thigh.

The men moved in a shuffling circle, their buckskin moccasins kicking up puffs of white dust. Their movements were accompanied by a chant, a low, humming sound that rose and fell like wind. With this came the rattling of the tortoise shells, not unlike the noise a rattlesnake makes when it shakes the horny, hinged buttons at the end of its tail.

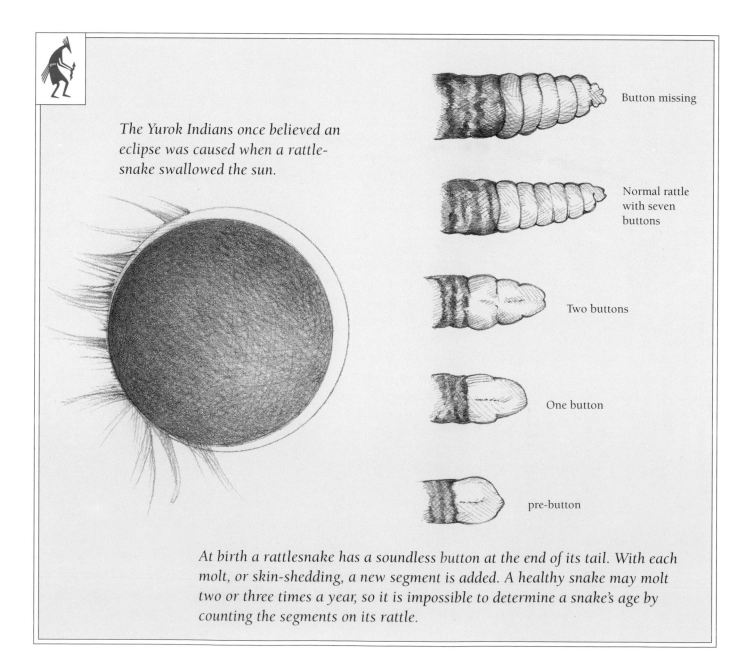

The Yurok Indians once believed an eclipse was caused when a rattlesnake swallowed the sun.

Button missing

Normal rattle with seven buttons

Two buttons

One button

pre-button

At birth a rattlesnake has a soundless button at the end of its tail. With each molt, or skin-shedding, a new segment is added. A healthy snake may molt two or three times a year, so it is impossible to determine a snake's age by counting the segments on its rattle.

After several turns around the dance area, a few of the dancers reached into a hole in the ground, a pit that had a shelter of cottonwood boughs over it. They came up with serpents in their hands. They gave these to other dancers, who put them in their mouths and carried them that way, moving in rhythm with the chant.

The soft insides of a rattlesnake are protected from rough ground and sharp rocks by scales made of keratin. This is the same material claws and fingernails are made of. A snake's scales create a durable shield between its internal organs and the outside world.

An early word for rattlesnakes was cascabel, *which means "bells" in Spanish. Cascabel came from the attempts of sixteenth-century explorers to describe the noise a rattlesnake makes when it shakes its rattle: "like the ringing of bells."*

Dancers with snakes were followed by men with prayer wands decorated with eagle feathers. The sticks were waved in the faces of the snakes, as if to distract them.

Many of the snakes were coachwhips, bull snakes, and other harmless reptiles. Some were full-grown rattlesnakes, their rattles buzzing furiously.

The dancers with snakes circled the plaza one-and-a-half times and then traded their snakes for fresh ones. During the exchange some snakes dropped to the ground and tried to wriggle away.

Young boys, ten or eleven years old, chased the loose snakes. They gathered them up and returned them to the hole in the earth. None got away.

For a long time I kept my eyes on one dancer, a short, stocky man with hair that flew up when he moved. As he made his circle he faced me for as long as a minute. He came close, and I could plainly see the sun shining on the scales of the snakes he carried. On one turn he had a rattlesnake in his mouth.

I stared in horror as the snake arched itself around and attached its jaws to the dancer's cheek. The man went on dancing.

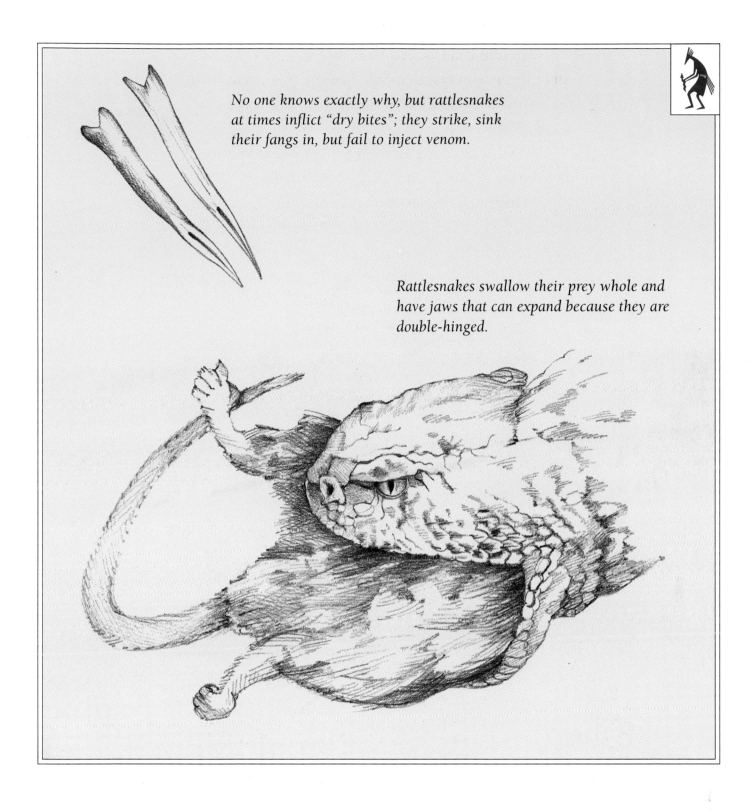

No one knows exactly why, but rattlesnakes at times inflict "dry bites"; they strike, sink their fangs in, but fail to inject venom.

Rattlesnakes swallow their prey whole and have jaws that can expand because they are double-hinged.

When it came time to change snakes, the man following with the prayer stick unhooked the rattlesnake's mouth from the dancer's face. Two spots of blood remained.

"Did you see?" I asked my father in a whisper. "Did you see what that snake did?"

"Quiet," my father said. "No talking now."

Later, when the dance was over, the two of us sat in the cab of the truck watching fat drops of rain spatter the windshield.

We had planned to stay another night but were rained out of our camp in the arroyo. Heavy rain, the kind Navajo Indians call "male rain," pounded the desert soil. The air smelled sweet from a mixture of wetness and dust. Night was coming. It was getting dark.

"Did you see what that rattlesnake did? How it bit the dancer on the cheek?"

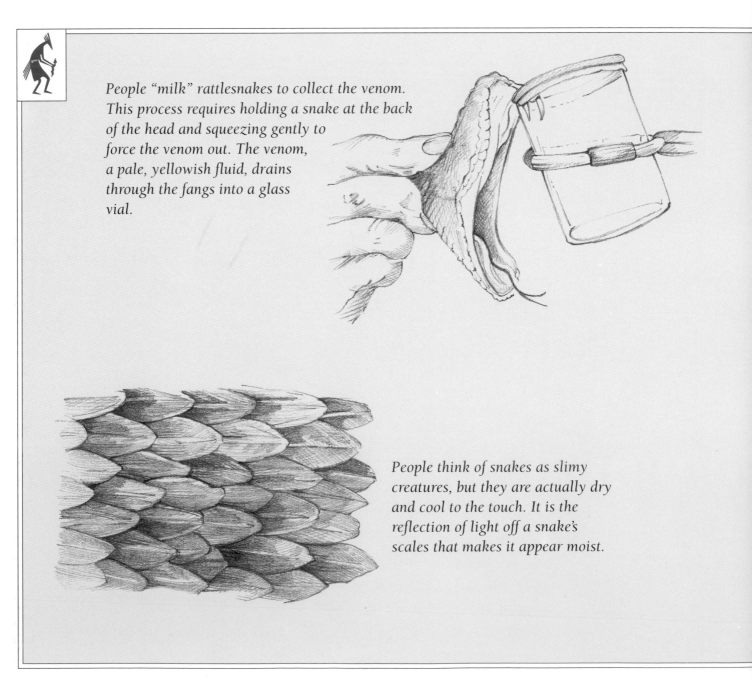

People "milk" rattlesnakes to collect the venom. This process requires holding a snake at the back of the head and squeezing gently to force the venom out. The venom, a pale, yellowish fluid, drains through the fangs into a glass vial.

People think of snakes as slimy creatures, but they are actually dry and cool to the touch. It is the reflection of light off a snake's scales that makes it appear moist.

"Yes," my father said. "I saw it. It's a mystery, how they do it. Nobody knows if it's magic or if they take the fangs out. Some say they 'milk' the venom out of the rattlesnakes, leaving the snakes harmless."

"If the Hopi honor snakes, they wouldn't pull out a rattler's fangs, because then it couldn't hunt. It would die of starvation."

"That's true," my father said. "The Hopi spend more than a week preparing for the dance. They wash the snakes, pray over them, and bless them. Maybe by the

Rattlesnakes are good swimmers. While in the water, they keep their rattles high and dry. Even when swimming, they are able to strike.

The Chiricahua Apache dread rattlesnakes. When they come upon one they call it "Mother" or "Mother's Mother" to show their respect for it and to express their desire to pass by unharmed.

time the men carry the snakes in their mouths, they've calmed them. Perhaps the dancers have a special way with snakes. The Hopi are protective of their rituals. There are questions we can't answer, because we're not Hopi."

We drove across a desert obscured by sheets of rain. My mind returned to what I'd seen that afternoon.

Figures of Hopi dancers, snakes of all kinds dangling from their mouths, passed through my imagination like the rain sweeping across the land. I believed the Hopi kept mysterious secrets in their hearts, knowledge of how to cajole a rattlesnake into withholding its venom.

Rattlesnake enemies are humans, hawks, eagles, pigs, weasels, king snakes, roadrunners, and great horned owls.

great horned owl

roadrunner

eagle

pig

For that day, at least, I knew the Hopi urged the reptiles they danced with to carry messages to the spirits. The drops of rain skidding over the hood of the truck proved it. The power of the Hopi dancers was equal to that of the rain-bringing spirits, and so the rain came.

THE RATTLESNAKE DANCE

I first saw the dance on an early morning walk in Wyoming. I was on a high, sage-covered plain when I came across two male prairie rattlesnakes.

Each snake was about three feet long. The two of them were on a clear area of sandy soil, circling as if they were facing off for battle.

In fact, it *was* a battle of sorts that was about to begin.

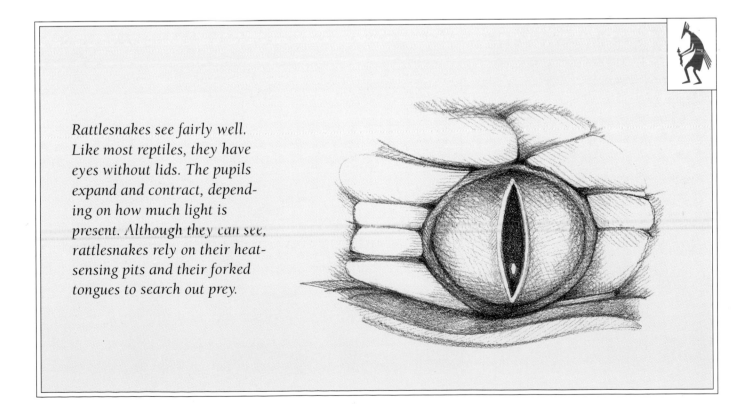

Rattlesnakes see fairly well. Like most reptiles, they have eyes without lids. The pupils expand and contract, depending on how much light is present. Although they can see, rattlesnakes rely on their heat-sensing pits and their forked tongues to search out prey.

Early settlers in the West who witnessed the rattlesnake dance told their neighbors they'd seen one snake eating another. Many of these people believed rattlesnakes swallowed each other at the same time, forming a hoop that got smaller and smaller with each passing minute.

The flicking of a rattlesnake's tongue is more than hypnotic, it is part of the animal's means of smelling and tasting. When the tongue goes out, it picks up specks of invisible matter in the air. Inside the mouth, the tongue passes over two holes lined with nerve cells. The holes are called the Jacobson's organ. Smell and taste information is sent through the Jacobson's organ to the snake's brain.

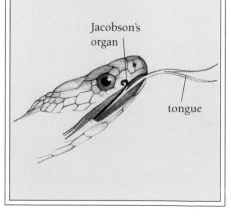

Jacobson's organ

tongue

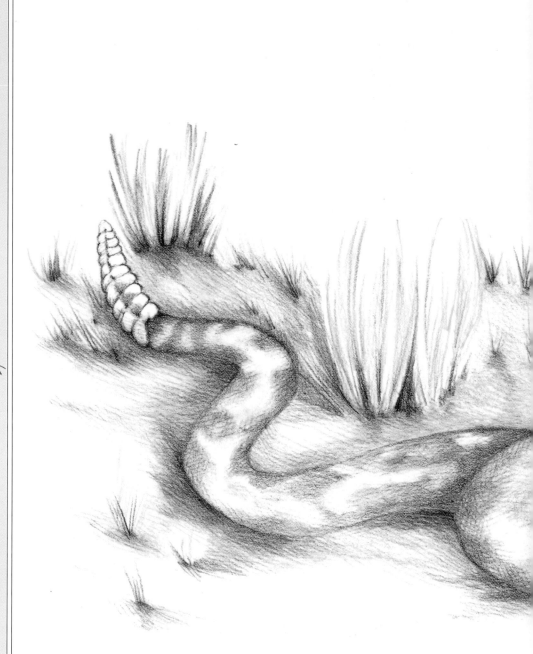

The distance between the two snakes narrowed until they were side by side and nearly touching. Neither snake appeared to be aware of my presence. I kept myself partly hidden behind a sagebrush while I watched.

The snakes reared up, lifting their scaled, muscular lengths into the air, their coiled tails giving them ground support.

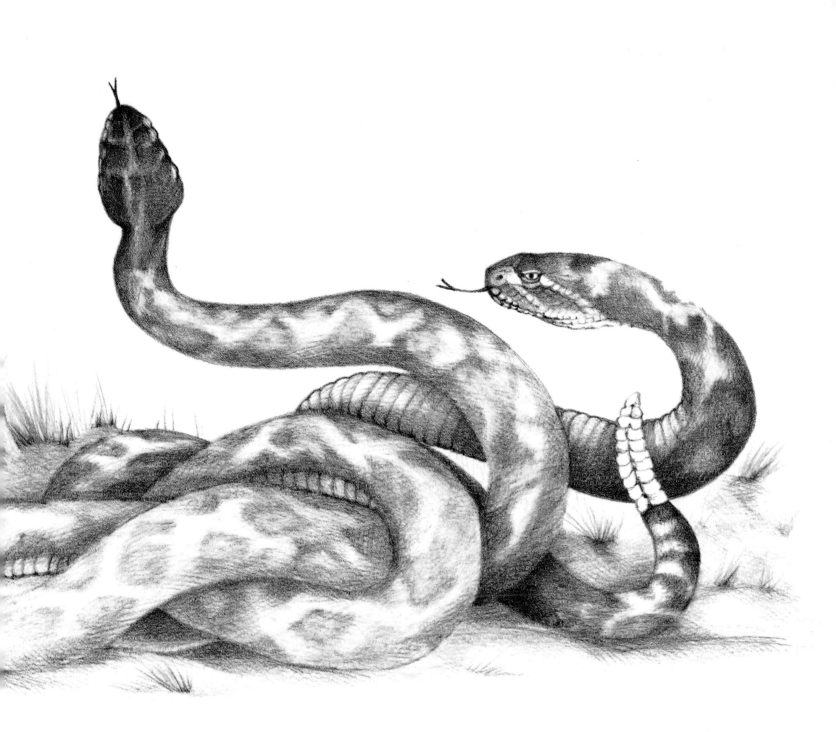

One of the snakes was thicker than the other. It coiled around its opponent until the two looked like a single twist of rope.

They pulled apart and met chin to chin, making me think of children on a playground ready for a fistfight.

With scales gleaming in the sun, the serpent rivals swung to and fro, embracing and then separating. They lowered their bodies to the ground and slid along with only a few inches between them. They gradually entwined, lacing themselves together. They stayed in this position for a long moment before they started to unwind.

With arched necks and tongues flicking, the snakes backed away from each other. As if in agreement about which move came next, the two snakes once more rose into the air.

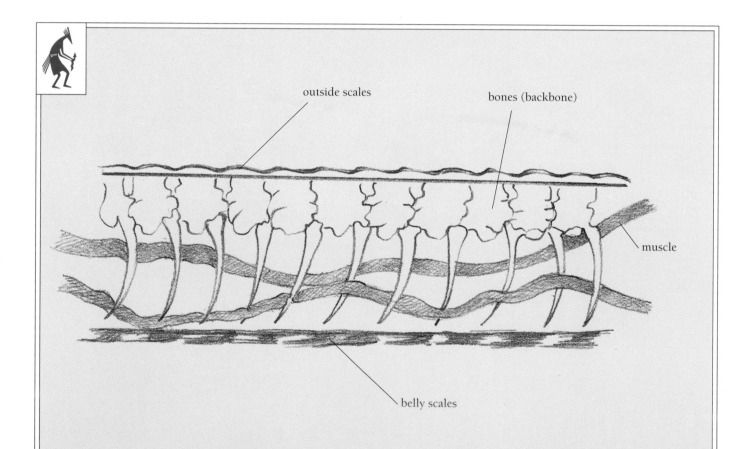

outside scales

bones (backbone)

muscle

belly scales

Rattlesnakes have small brains enclosed in a boxy, bony skull. The length of a snake's body is made up of three layers, beginning with soft, fibrous tissue covering internal organs. Next are muscles with pigment in them. This is the layer that gives the snake its colors. Last are the keratin scales, which overlap like roof tiles. The internal organs of a rattlesnake are the same as any animal's with a backbone, except they are elongated to fit a snake's narrow body.

The display went on for close to two hours. When the end came, it was sudden and unexpected.

The thicker snake elevated itself above the other and in a move almost too quick to see, slammed its body down, hitting the thinner snake hard and knocking it to the ground.

The first illustration of a rattlesnake appeared in a book written by Francisco Hernandez in 1628. The book is a natural history of Mexico. In his description of the rattlesnake, Hernandez called it la señora de las serpeientes, *or, "the mother of all serpents."*

The loser did not rise. It kept still for about three minutes and then slithered away in an S-curve motion.

I decided to follow.

I found the snake lying under a sagebrush. Its head went up at my approach, but it did not buzz its warning sound. There were no wounds on its body. The two snakes had acted out their combat with no biting, striking, or intent to kill.

In truth, the rattlesnake dance is a wrestling match that male snakes carry out with a single objective — one of the two is eventually knocked to the ground and "defeated." The winning male is likely to mate with a receptive female while the loser may spend as long as two weeks isolated from other rattlesnakes.

It is bewildering that animals with such tiny brains, clearly driven by instinct and not thought, act out a ritual as graceful as a ballet dance, a mock combat with no physical injury.

Rattlesnakes are fascinating animals. They inspire awe, fear, curiosity, and nearly endless speculation. How do the Hopi handle deadly snakes with no ill effects? How do male rattlesnakes know what moves to make when they dance? And how did I survive snakebite as a child?

I'll probably never know the answers to these questions. Rattlesnakes remain as mysterious and amazing to me now as they were to our ancestors of long ago — and as they were to me as a child.